Strategic Paper P9
Management Accounting - Financial Strategy

GW00706116

First edition 2005
Second edition January 2006

ISBN 0 7517 2516 1 (previous edition ISBN 0 7517 1969 2)

British Library Cataloguing-in-Publication Data

A catalogue record for this book is available from the British Library

Published by

BPP Professional Education, Aldine House, Aldine Place, London W12 8AW

www.bpp.com

Printed in Great Britain by Ashford Colour Press

Welcome to BPP's CIMA **Passcards** for **Strategic Paper P9 Management Accounting: Financial Strategy.**

- They **focus on your exam** and **save you time**.

- They incorporate **diagrams** to kick start your memory.

- They follow the overall **structure** of the BPP Study Texts, but BPP's CIMA **Passcards** are not just a condensed book. Each card has been separately designed for clear presentation. Topics are self contained and can be grasped visually.

- CIMA **Passcards** are still **just the right size** for pockets, briefcases and bags.

- CIMA **Passcards** should be used in conjunction with the revision plan in the front pages of the Kit. The plan identifies key questions for you to try in the Kit.

Run through the **Passcards** as often as you can during your final revision period. The day before the exam, try to go through the **Passcards** again! You will then be well on your way to passing your exams.

Good luck!

Contents

1: Objectives of organisations

Topic List

Objectives

Stakeholders

Agency and goal congruence

Publicly-owned and
non-commercial bodies

Financial management decisions

Don't forget that this is an exam about business awareness as well as technical issues. A favourite exam question is to ask you to discuss which of a choice of actions is preferable and you need to consider the business's specific objectives to be able to do this effectively.

Financial objectives

The main objective is maximisation of profits to maximise shareholder wealth and company valuation. Other financial targets might include:

- Level of gearing
- Profit retentions
- Operating profitability
- Cash generation
- Value added

There may be conflicts between multiple financial objectives, or between short-term and long-term objectives. Companies should also consider how **efficiently** the profits are being generated and what **volume of investment** has been required to earn profits.

Non-financial objectives

- Welfare of employees
- Welfare of management, perks, benefits in kind
- Welfare of society, eg green policies
- Provision of certain level of service
- Responsibilities towards customers/suppliers

Valuation methods

- Balance sheet/going concern basis
- Break-up basis
- Market values

Stakeholders

Groups or individuals having a legitimate interest in the organisation's activities

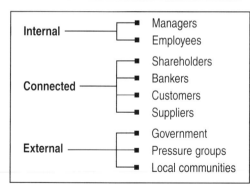

Internal — Managers, Employees

Connected — Shareholders, Bankers, Customers, Suppliers

External — Government, Pressure groups, Local communities

Shareholders

Shareholders are often distant from the day-to-day running of the company.

Having a large number of shareholders (quoted/some public companies) has some implications.

- Greater market for shares
- Less likelihood of controlling interest
- Less effect on share price if one shareholder sells
- Easy to frustrate takeover
- High administrative costs
- Different shareholder objectives/tax position

Managers need to understand shareholder attitudes to dividends v capital gains and desirable levels of risk.

Agency theory

proposes that, whilst individual team members act in their own self-interest, individual well-being depends on the well-being of other individuals and on the performance of the team.

Corporations are set of contracts between principals (suppliers of finance) and agents (management).

The agency problem

If managers don't have significant shareholdings, what stops them under-performing and over-rewarding themselves?

Goal congruence

is accordance between the objectives of agents acting within an organisation and the objectives of the organisation as a whole.

Goal congruence can be achieved by giving managers incentives related to profit or share price.

- Profit-related pay
- Rights to subscribe at reduced price
- Executive share-option plans

Shareholder value analysis may help managers concentrate on value-adding activities rather than short-term profits.

State-owned industries

Financial objectives will be sub-ordinated to political and social objectives, to provide a socially vital service or a certain standard of service. However state-owned industries will be expected to achieve a certain rate of return.

Financial management in nationalised industries

- Strategic objectives
- Investment plans and appraisal
- Corporate plans, targets and aims
- External financing limits

Non profit-making organisations

These exist to provide services, but face the financial constraints of obtaining funds.

Funds should be used:

- Economically
- Efficiently
- Effectively (Value for money)

Executive agencies

Agencies that carry out certain services are answerable to the government, but are also independent. Targets include financial performance, output, service and quality and efficiency.

Investment decisions

Investment decisions include:

- New projects
- Takeovers
- Mergers
- Sell-off/Divestment

The financial manager must:

- Identify decisions
- Evaluate them
- Decide optimal funding

Financing decisions

Financial decisions include:

- Long-term capital structure

Need to determine source, cost and risk of long-term finance.

- Short-term working capital management

Balance between profitability and liquidity is crucial.

Dividend decisions

Dividend decisions may affect views of the company's long-term prospects, and thus the shares' market values.

Payment of dividends limits the amount of retained earnings available for re-investment.

Consider interaction of decisions, eg paying out **dividends** leaves less funds available to **finance investments**.

2: Constraints on financial strategy

Topic List

As part of your background reading for this paper, be aware of press coverage on the constraints covered in this chapter affect organisations in different sectors.

Internal constraints

- Limiting factors, eg shortage of production capacity
- Owners lack financial resources
- Owners unwilling to take on debt commitments
- Need to fulfil investor requirements
- Consistency with business strategy

Corporate governance

Corporate governance is the system by which companies are directed and controlled. It covers directors' responsibilities, the way decisions are made, financial responsibilities and relations with investors and auditors.

Other requirements

- Audit committees supervise relations with auditors + review systems
- Need for internal audit function
- Clear disclosures - corporate governance, performance, internal controls, remuneration

Directors

- Boards should meet regularly
- Division of responsibilities
- Committees - audit, nomination, remuneration
- Balance of executive + non-executive
- Limits on service contracts

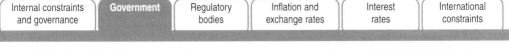

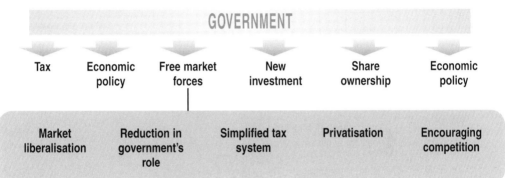

GOVERNMENT

| Tax | Economic policy | Free market forces | New investment | Share ownership | Economic policy |

| Market liberalisation | Reduction in government's role | Simplified tax system | Privatisation | Encouraging competition |

The government also regulates private markets where these fail to bring about an efficient use of resources. Ways of influencing government policy include initial involvement, comments, lobbying and assisting in enforcement.

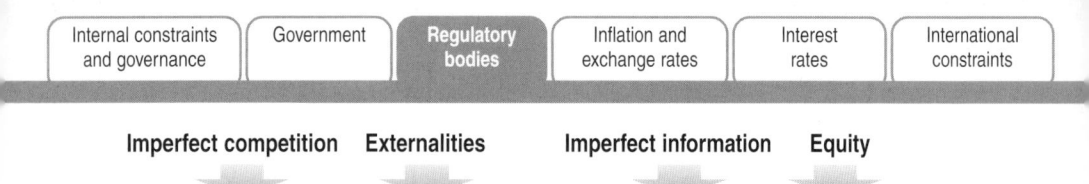

Imperfect competition   **Externalities**   **Imperfect information**   **Equity**

REGULATION

Price control   **Profit control**   **Competition promotion**   **Quality and safety**   **Social implications**

Costs of regulation

- Enforcement costs - costs of agency and costs to regulated
- Regulatory capture - regulator increasingly acts in regulated's interests
- Unintended consequences - investment in costly capital processes if profits are limited

Deregulation

The removal of regulations to increase the impact of free market forces. More competition may have negative consequences.

- Loss of economies of scale
- Worse service

Effects of inflation

- ↑ costs of production

- ↑ selling prices

- ↑ interest rates to dampen demand

- ↓ foreign exchange rates (through purchasing power parity)

- ↓ demand (through higher prices/uncertainty)

Effects of exchange rate increases

- ↑ costs of exports
- ↓ costs of imports
- ↑ value of investments in UK

Exchange rate policies

- Fixed
- Floating
- Managed float

Business and exchange rates

Business want certainty, but also an exchange rate that means that they are competitive. Exchange rate uncertainty can lead to businesses financing investments abroad by borrowing in the same currency.

2: Constraints on financial strategy

Reasons why interest rates differ

- Risk
- Need to make profit on re-lending
- Duration of lending
- Size of loan
- International interest rates
- Different types of financial asset

Nominal and real rates of interest

Real rate of interest $= \dfrac{1 + \text{nominal rate of interest}}{1 + \text{rate of inflation}} - 1$

Effects of interest rate increase

- Market value of interest-bearing securities falls
- Return expected from shares rises
- Price of shares falls
- Companies reduce total debt finance
- Companies raise new debt finance by short-term borrowing/debt at variable interest rate
- Companies with surplus cash switch into interest-bearing securities
- Required return on capital investments rises

Upward sloping yield curve

- Compensate investor for tying up money

- Greater risk in lending long-term

Reverse yield gap

Yields lower on shares than low-risk debt, reflects desire for capital gains.

Downward sloping yield curve

- Interest rates expected to fall

- Government influence

- Investors confined to one segment

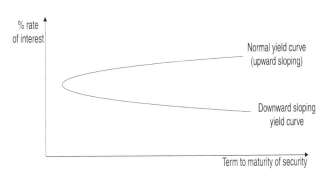

2: Constraints on financial strategy

Government action

- Quotas, limiting quantities
- Tariffs, making imports more expensive
- Legal standards
- Restrictions on foreign ownership
- Nationalisation
- Minimum shareholding by residents

Limiting effects of political risk

- Negotiate concessions
- Export credit insurance
- Location of production/distribution overseas
- Patents
- Making local institutions dependent
- Joint ventures
- Use of management charges

Blocked funds

Blocked funds arise from restrictions on types of transaction for which payments abroad allowed. Avoidance measures include sales of goods and services, royalty and management charges.

Other constraints

- Adverse foreign exchange movements
- Geographical separation
- Risk of litigation

3: Performance analysis and forecasting

Topic List

Ratio analysis

Information in accounts

Cash forecasts

Forecast financial statements

For this paper, you must be able to choose the appropriate measures and indicators of an organisation's situation, and discuss whether these indicate that the organisation has met its objectives.

You may also be asked to prepare forecast financial statements as well as forecast cash flow statements, and consider how different policies affect forecasts.

Remember!

Consider carefully the requirements of the question and the contents of the scenario before calculating ratios. The examiner will be looking for relevant ratios accompanied by meaningful comments.

Profitability and return

- Return on capital employed
- Profit margin
- Asset turnover

Liquidity ratios

- Current ratio
- Inventory turnover
- Receivables days
- Acid test ratio
- Payables days

Debt and gearing

- Debt ratio (Total debts: Assets)
- Gearing (Proportion of debt in long-term capital)
- Interest cover
- Cash flow ratio (Cash inflow: Total debts)

Stock market ratios

- Dividend yield
- Earnings per share
- Price/earnings ratio
- Interest yield
- Dividend cover

Comparisons with previous years

- % growth in profit
- Sales
- Changes in gearing ratio
- Changes in current/quick ratios
- Changes in asset turnover
- Changes in EPS, market price, dividend

Comparisons with other companies in same industry

These can put improvements into perspective if other companies are doing better, and provide evidence of general trends.

- Growth rates
- Retained profits
- Non-current asset levels

Comparisons with companies in different industries

Investors need to know differences between sectors.

- Sales growth
- Profit
- ROCE
- P/E ratios
- Dividend yields

Problems with ratio analysis

- Use of comparable information
- Out-of-date information
- Ratios not definitive

- Careful interpretation
- Manipulation
- Comparisons with other information

- Valuation methods
- Asset age and nature

Non-current assets

- New share issue
- Level of profits retained
- Scrip issues/dividends

Share capital and reserves

- Redeemable debt
- Earn-out arrangements (see below)
- Potential/contingent liabilities

Financial obligations

ACCOUNTING INFORMATION

Loans

- Whether loans secured
- Closeness of redemption/repayment date
- Interest rates

Contingencies

- Guarantees
- Uncalled share liabilities
- Lawsuits and claims

Post balance sheet events

- Mergers/acquisitions
- Asset sales
- New/closed trading activities

Earn-out arrangement

is where owners/managers selling an organisation receive part of their consideration linked to business's performance after the sale.

- Initial provision of minimum amount guaranteed
- Further provisions as more data is available
- Difficult to make reliable estimates for a long time
- Must take uncertainties into account

Segmental analysis

Disclosure by class of business or geographical area.

Private Finance Initiative

is where the private sector provides a long-term service to the public sector in return for a payment covering the use of any assets involved, and the cost of any ancillary services provided.

PFI transactions include:

- Services sold to public sector
- Fees through direct charges
- Joint ventures

Corporate failure models

Z-scores use ratios. Argenti's model focuses on defects, mistakes and symptoms.

Receipts and payments	Adjustments to profit (working capital/depreciation)	Balance sheet based forecast	IAS 7 format
⬇	⬇	⬇	⬇

CASH FORECASTS

⬇	⬇	⬇	⬇
Amount required	When required	Period required	Whether available

Balance sheet based forecast

The increase or decrease in funds is the balancing figure. Forecasts used as:

- Longer-term strategic estimates

- Check on realism of cash flow based forecasts

A forecast cash flow can also be derived from the profit and loss account and balance sheet.

Quality control of forecasts

Accuracy and relevance of forecasts should be checked by reviewing actual cash flows against forecasts and preparing updated rolling forecasts.

	£	£
Intangible assets (current figures)		X
Tangible assets (estimate purchases/sales)		X
Inventory ⎫ (Same as current/	X	
Receivables ⎬ % increase or decrease)	X	X
Trade payables (as receivables/inventory)	(X)	
Bank loans (not overdrafts)	(X)	
Tax (estimate)	(X)	
Dividends (estimate)	(X)	(X)
Long-term liabilities		(X)
		Y
Share capital (same)		X
Profit + loss (estimate increase)		X
Other reserves (same)		X
		Z

Y - Z = Funding shortfall (positive)   Surplus (negative)

Forecast financial statements

Forecast financial statements may be prepared in conjunction with cash flow forecasts to see if the company is likely to meet stated financial objectives.

Assumptions may be made on:

- Sales/cost increases
- Accounting ratios
- Fixed asset purchases
- Dividends
- Working capital levels

Consider also carrying out sensitivity analysis on effect of changes in economic and business variables.

Taking action

Business with **potential liquidity problems** can sell investments, tighten working capital control or borrow. If the need to borrow is known in advance, favourable rates may be obtained. Businesses with **surplus cash** can use forecasts to help them decide how best to invest it. Interest earnings may be significant.

4: Financial strategies

This chapter lists the most important factors you should consider when assessing alternative financial strategies for an organisation.

With dividends, you may be asked to consider the effect on earnings of different dividend policies, or how different kinds of shareholders are affected by dividend policy.

For financial reporting issues, concentrate on the effects on financial strategy.

Clarity

- Clear benefits of strategy
- Activities directed to benefits
- Financial resources specified
- Contingency plans if environment changes
- Long-term implications

Acceptability

Strategy must be acceptable to key stakeholders, including acceptable risks.

Shareholders must be convinced that wealth targets will be met.

Lenders must be convinced commitments will be met.

Feasibility

Organisation should demonstrate it has sufficient resources (finance, materials, technology) and be able to generate enough returns to compensate resource suppliers. Also can the organisation fuflil any conditions that might be imposed on it?

Suitability

Financial strategy should be compatible with business strategy. It should be directed towards improving competitive position, exploiting strengths and grasping opportunities.

Dividends

In practice directors determine dividends, shareholders can vote to reduce recommended dividends, but not increase them. Directors may favour retaining earnings as:

- Retained cash can be used to finance investments without involving investors/outsiders

- No costs

- Avoids possibility of change of control

As market lacks information about underlying cash flows, dividends provide signal of prospects

- Consistent dividend policy

- Preferably steady growth

- May be used to defend a takeover

Practical aspects

- Need to remain profitable

- Law on distributable profits

- Dividend restraints imposed by loan agreements

- Effect of inflation

- Need to retain some profits to maintain operating capability

- Limit level of gearing

- Need for ready cash to pay dividends

- Other sources of available finance

Modigliani and Miller

M&M argue that the level of dividends is irrelevant, that shareholders will be indifferent between a new investment being funded by a cut in dividend or new equity finance. The theory assumes:

- No tax

- No transaction costs

- All relevant information available

M&M argue that if a dividend is paid, shares will suffer loss in value equal to dividend because of the need to obtain (and reward) outside finance. Shareholders can 'manufacture' own dividends through selling shares.

Arguments against M&M

- Different tax rates on dividends/capital gains affect shareholder preferences

- Companies prefer earnings retention if capital is rationed

- Imperfect markets mean shareholders want high dividends as funds for further investment

- Transaction costs make selling shares less attractive

- Limits on available information lead to companies maintaining dividend levels to retain members' confidence

Share re-purchase

Share re-purchase can be from distributable profits or new issue proceeds. A private company can purchase its own shares out of capital.

Benefits	Disadvantages
☑ Use for surplus cash	☒ Determination of purchase price
☑ Increase in earnings per share	☒ No better use of funds
☑ Increase in gearing	☒ Tax disadvantage for shareholders
☑ Prevention of takeover	

Scrip dividend

is a dividend in the form of new shares.

- Means of retaining funds
- Enhanced scrip dividends more valuable than cash alternative

Scrip issue

is the issue of new shares in proportion to existing holdings, reducing retained earnings. It is also known as a bonus issue.

| **Risk management** | **Staff motivation** | **Increased profits** | **Good citizen** |

Environmental accounting

| **Costs of outputs** | **Waste and pollution avoidance** | **Product environmental life cycle** | **Budgeting** |

Environmental reporting

- Impact of activities upon environment
- Environmental objectives
- Monitoring progress
- Assessment of success
- Independent verification

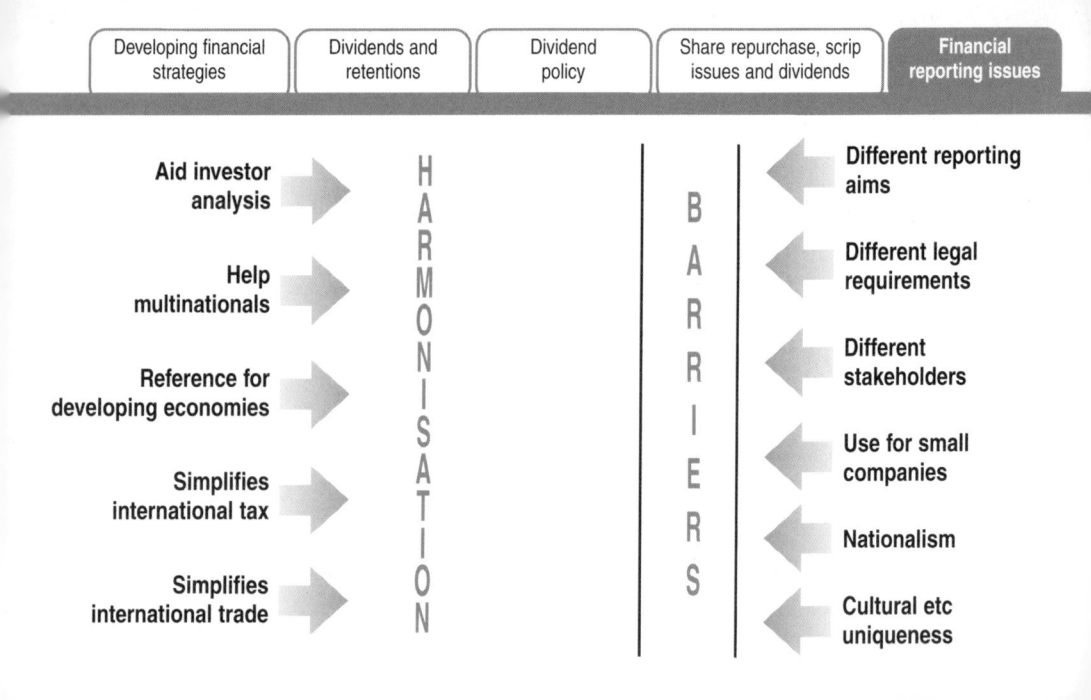

H A R M O N I S A T I O N

Aid investor analysis →

Help multinationals →

Reference for developing economies →

Simplifies international tax →

Simplifies international trade →

B A R R I E R S

← Different reporting aims

← Different legal requirements

← Different stakeholders

← Use for small companies

← Nationalism

← Cultural etc uniqueness

Introducing international accounting standards

- Realistic assessment of resources required

- Detailed task planning

- Proper staffing

- Sufficient IT resources

- Full training

- Continuous monitoring

- Celebration of achievements

- Follow-up procedures

As well as considering the short-term implications, organisations should plan implementation of the long-term changes to systems and processes that will be needed.

Share-based payments

IFRS 2 requires organisations to reflect in their income statement effects of share-based payments. Effect may be to make employee share plans less popular, as companies are having to account for the full economic consequences.

Other criticisms:

- True cost is to shareholders through dilution

- True cost is value of services

- Double EPS impact (dilution of shares + reduction of profits)

- Unnecessarily complicated provisions

Human resource accounting

UK government task force emphasised that activity needs to be measured in order to be properly managed, and investors require information on human capital.

Advantages

- ☑ Supports strategic decision-making
- ☑ Indicates strategic success and potential for high performance
- ☑ Increasingly popular
- ☑ Sign of greater corporate openness

Disadvantages

- ☒ Lack of obvious shareholder benefits
- ☒ No obvious best practice
- ☒ Measures give limited information
- ☒ Confidentiality concerns
- ☒ Mechanistic approach

Disclosures

Organisations should disclose how their human resource policies link with strategy and performance. Also disclose:

- Size and composition of workforce
- Employee motivation indicators
- Staff training and development
- Remuneration and employment
- Leadership and succession planning

5: Equity capital

Topic List

Stock market listing

Share issues

Rights and scrip issues

Preference shares

Warrants and euro-issues

*In this chapter we concentrate on equity share capital, issued share capital which does not carry preferential rights but which does have a residual interest in the asset of the equity after deducting liabilities. You may be asked which type of issue is **appropriate** for a particular company or to calculate issue or ex-rights price. Don't forget euro-issues for multi-national companies.*

Stock market listing

→ Access to wider pool of finance
→ Improved marketability of shares
→ Transfer of capital to other uses
→ Enhancement of company image
→ Facilitation of growth by acquisition

Disadvantages of obtaining listing

- Loss of control
- Vulnerability to takeover
- More scrutiny
- Greater restrictions on directors
- Compliance costs

Retained earnings

Obtaining cash by retaining funds within the business rather than paying dividends.

- Flexible source of finance
- Same pattern of shareholdings
- Opportunity costs of lost dividend income

Offer for sale

The company sells shares to the public at large. Offer for sale by tender means allotting shares at the highest price they will be taken up.

Costs of share issues
■ Underwriting costs
■ Stock Exchange listing fees
■ Issuing house, solicitors, auditors, public relation fees
■ Printing and distribution costs
■ Advertising

Placing

Placing means arranging for most of an issue to be bought by a small number of institutional investors. It is cheaper than an offer for sale.

Pricing share issues
■ Price of similar companies
■ Current market conditions
■ Future trading prospects
■ Premium on launch
■ Price growth after launch
■ Higher price means fewer shares and less earnings dilution

5: Equity capital

Rights issue

is an offer to existing shareholders enabling them to buy new shares.

Offer price will be lower than current market price

Advantages of rights issue

- Lower issue costs than offer for sale
- Shareholders acquire shares at discount
- Relative voting rights unaffected

Scrip dividend

is a dividend payment in the form of new shares, not cash.

Scrip issue/bonus issue

is an issue of new shares to current shareholders, by converting equity reserves.

Value of rights

Theoretical ex-rights price – Issue price

Theoretical ex-rights price

$\frac{1}{N+1} ((N \times \text{cum rights price}) + \text{issue price})$ **Exam formula**

where N = number of shares required to buy one new share

Preference shares

are shares which have a fixed percentage dividend, payable in priority to any dividend paid to ordinary shareholders. They can only be paid if sufficient distributable profits are available.

- Participating preference shares have entitlement in addition to their specified rate
- Cumulative preference shares have right carried forward to later years

Advantages

- ✓ Dividends not paid when profits poor
- ✓ Don't dilute voting rights
- ✓ Lower gearing
- ✓ Don't restrict borrowing power
- ✓ No shareholder right to appoint receiver

Disadvantages

- ✗ Dividend payments not tax-deductible
- ✗ Not popular with investors (can't be secured on assets, low dividend yield)
- ✗ Loan stock ranks higher in liquidation
- ✗ Issue costs more expensive than for debentures

Warrants

are rights for an investor to subscribe for new shares at a future date at a fixed pre-determined price (the exercise price). Warrants are usually issued with unsecured loan stock.

Features of warrants

- Don't involve interest/dividends
- Make loan stock issue more attractive
- Don't immediately dilute EPS
- Income in form of capital gains
- Low investor outlay/maybe high profit

Price of warrants

During exercise period, price shouldn't fall below higher of nil and the theoretical value.

$$\text{Theoretical value} = (\text{Current share price} - \text{Exercise price}) \times \text{No of shares from each warrant}$$

Euro-equity issues

Issues of equity in market outside a company's domestic market:

- Raise more funds
- Attract wider shareholding base
- Less regulation
- Reduced foreign exchange risk

6: Debt finance

Topic List

Bank loans

Loan capital

Debentures

Convertibles

International debt

Lenders' assessment

You may be asked as part of a question to discuss the main features and advantages and disadvantages of certain types of loan finance.

Overdrafts and loans

Overdrafts are used for short-term financing needs. A maximum facility is granted; the bank will want any long-term balance reduced. Overdrafts are repayable on demand; security may be specific assets or over the whole business.

Loans are medium and long-term. The organisation won't be subject to the publicity requirements or costs of a loan stock issue on the stock exchange. Security or restrictive covenants may be imposed.

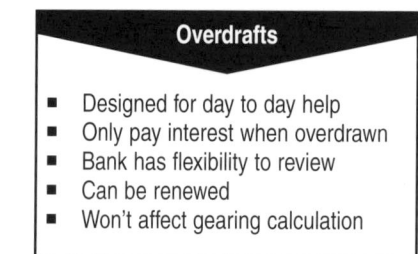

Overdrafts

- Designed for day to day help
- Only pay interest when overdrawn
- Bank has flexibility to review
- Can be renewed
- Won't affect gearing calculation

Overdrafts

v

loans

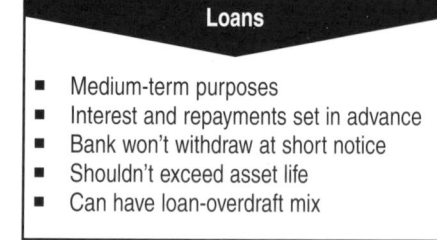

Loans

- Medium-term purposes
- Interest and repayments set in advance
- Bank won't withdraw at short notice
- Shouldn't exceed asset life
- Can have loan-overdraft mix

Loan stock

The stock has a nominal value, the debt owed by the company, and interest is paid on this amount. Security may be given.

> **Fixed charge** (specific assets, can't dispose without lender's consent)
>
> **Floating charge** (class of assets, can dispose until default)

Deep discount bonds are issued at a large discount to nominal value of stock.

Zero coupon bonds are issued at a discount, with no interest paid on them.

Redemption

> Redemption is repayment of loan stock.
>
> Value of redeemable debt =
>
> (Interest earnings × Annuity factor) + (Redemption value × DCF factor)

Value of irredeemable debt

$$P_0 = \frac{i(1-t)}{k_{dnet}}$$ **Exam formula**

$i(1-t)$ is annual tax after interest

k_{dnet} is after tax cost of debt

Debentures

are the written acknowledgement of debt including provisions about interest payment and capital repayment. The trust deed allows trustees to intervene in the event of breaches. The market price of debentures depends on coupon rate relative to market rates.

Advantages of debt

- ✓ Interest tax-deductible
- ✓ Can offer security
- ✓ Rank above shares in liquidation
- ✓ Issue costs lower than for shares
- ✓ No change in control
- ✓ Lenders don't participate in profits

Disadvantages of debt

- ✗ Interest must be paid each year
- ✗ Funds required for redemption or repayment
- ✗ Increased financial risk for ordinary shareholders
- ✗ Shareholders may demand higher return
- ✗ Articles or covenants restrict borrowing

Convertibles

are fixed return equities convertible at pre-determined rates and at holder's option into ordinary shares at a pre-determined price. Conversion premium is the difference between the issue value of stock and conversion value at issue date. Companies aim to issue stock with **greatest possible conversion premium**. Convertibles normally have lower rate of return than straight debt, the price investors pay for conversion rights.

Advantages of debt

- ✓ Sweetener for debt
- ✓ Lower interest than straight debt
- ✓ Conversion rights substitute for other lender conditions
- ✓ Equity issued at higher price than current price
- ✓ Possibility of forced conversion
- ✓ Issue costs not required on conversion

Disadvantages of debt

- ✗ Issuer loses out if market price of shares is above conversion price
- ✗ Debt may have to be repaid
- ✗ Borrowers reluctant to invest due to lower yield
- ✗ No extra funds if conversion takes place

6: Debt finance

Eurocurrency markets

Deposit of funds with bank outside the country of origin of funds and re-lending for short-term (three months).

Eurocurrency loans

UK company borrowing foreign currency from UK bank.

Syndicated credits

Borrowing facility which may not be used in full. Relatively high rates of interest. Used to fund takeovers/major debt repayments.

Eurocommercial paper

Short-term (< 1 year, generally 1 – 13 weeks) notes that can be sold in discount market.

- Interest rates determined by market conditions
- No rating
- Higher short-term investment gains

Eurobonds

are bonds issued in capital markets, denominated in a currency often differing from the country of issue and sold internationally.

Used by large, profitable multinationals:

- As long-term loans, to finance big capital expansion programmes

- When they require borrowing that is not subject to national exchange controls

- To avoid domestic capital issue regulations

Euromarkets v domestic markets

- Borrowing – lending spreads closer on Euromarket

- Euromarket loans don't normally need security

- Interest paid gross on Euromarkets

- Flexible drawn – down (redemption) dates

- Reduction in foreign exchange risk

- Lack of experience of overseas borrowing

- Borrowing in lower interest rate currency may have short-term advantages

- Easier to raise large sums on Euromarkets

P urpose
- → Finance new business
- → Business can realise purpose
- → Funding of working capital should be short-term

A mount
- → Reasonable estimate
- → If too much, may be used for different purpose
- → If too little, may need more later

R epayments
- → Terms clear
- → Sufficient income earned to meet payment

T erm
- → Appears appropriate
- → Consistent with income timestream

S ecurity
- → Adequate
- → If risk excessive, should not lend even with security

7: Securities markets and market efficiency

Topic List

Financial intermediation

Money and capital markets

Market analysis

Efficient market hypothesis

*In this chapter you need to learn what the different institutions and markets can offer businesses. You may be asked to make judgements on which sources of finance are **relevant** to a particular business. You may also have to explain the relevance of the level of market efficiency to a business decision.*

Financial intermediation

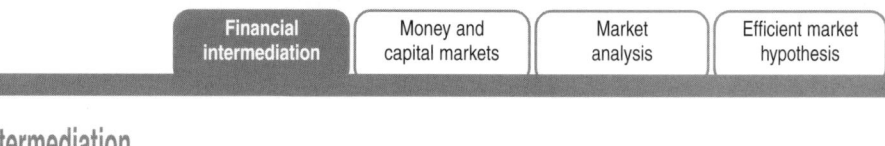

is the bringing together of providers and users of finance.

- Convenient means of saving money
- Aggregating of amounts lent for borrowing
- Pooling reduces risk
- Maturity transformation

Credit creation means expanding lending and deposit liabilities by more than the initial increase in banks' reserves.

Commercial banks

The retail (High Street) and wholesale banks

- Payments mechanism
- Wealth store
- Providers of funds

Merchant banks

- Share issue and underwriting
- Large scale lending
- Foreign exchange/bullion dealing
- Stock Exchange business
- Investment management
- Takeover/merger advice

Money markets

are operated by banks/financial institutions and provide means of trading, lending and borrowing in the short-term.

Capital markets

are markets for trading in long-term financial instruments, equities and debentures. They enable organisations to raise new finance, investors to realise investments and companies to merge/takeover.

- Primary or official
- Interbank
- Eurocurrency
- Certificate of deposit
- Local authority
- Finance house
- Inter-company

- Stock Exchanges
- UK's Alternative Investment Market (AIM)

Fundamental theory of share values

states that the value of a share will be the discounted present value of future expected dividends, discounted at shareholders' cost of capital.

In practice share prices are affected by day to day fluctuations reflecting:

- Supply and demand in particular period
- Investor confidence
- Market interest rate movements

Other 'irrational' reasons for movements include:

- Overreaction to recent events
- Neglect of individual shares/types of company

Formulae

P_0 is ex dividend value

$$= \frac{d}{k_e}$$

d is constant annual dividend in perpetuity

k_e is shareholders' cost of capital

$$P_0 = \frac{d_0(1+g)}{k_e - g} = \frac{d_1}{k_e - g}$$

d_0 is dividend in current year (year 0)

$d_0(1+g)/d_1$ is expected future dividend in year 1

Technical analysts or chartists

They work on the assumption that past price patterns will be repeated.

Analysis is based on trend reversals, certain signal points to buy or sell.

Random walks

This theory is consistent with fundamental theory, based on the idea of intrinsic value which alters as new information becomes available.

For irredeemable debt

$$P_0 = \frac{i(1-t)}{k_{d\,net}}$$

where P_0 is ex-interest value

$i\,(1-t)$ is after tax interest

$k_{d\,net}$ is net cost of debt

Without tax:

$$P_0 = \frac{i}{k_d}$$

Efficient market hypothesis

is the hypothesis that stock market reacts immediately to all available information. An investor cannot obtain higher than average returns from a well-diversified portfolio. The hypothesis is consistent with random walk theory and fundamental analysis.

- Price of securities bought and sold reflects all relevant information
- No individual dominates market
- Transaction costs do not discourage trading
- Investors are rational
- Costs of information acquisition are insignificant

Weak form efficiency	**Semi strong form efficiency**	**Strong form efficiency**
Prices reflect all relevant information about past price movements and their implications	Prices reflect: ■ Past price information ■ Publicly available knowledge	Prices reflect: ■ Past price changes ■ Public knowledge ■ Inside knowledge

8: Leasing

Topic List

In a question on leasing, you may be asked to assess a leasing decision from either the lessee's or lessor's viewpoint. You will also probably have to discuss the features and attractiveness of different types of leasing arrangements.

Leasing

is a contract between the lessor and lessee for the hire of a specific asset.

Hire purchase

is a form of instalment credit, where ownership passes to the customer on the payment of the final credit instalment (unlike leasing, lessee never becomes owner of goods).

Hire purchase payments consist of capital element (towards asset cost) and interest.

Leasing

- **Lessor** has ownership of asset
- **Lessee** has possession and ownership of asset on payment of specified rentals over period

Hire purchase

- Supplier sells goods to finance house
- Supplier delivers goods to customer who purchases them
- HP arrangement exists between finance house and customer

Operating leases

- Lessor bears most of risk and rewards
- Lessor responsible for servicing and maintenance
- Period of lease short, less than useful economic life of asset
- Asset not shown on lessee's balance sheet

Finance leases

- Lessee bears most of risks and rewards
- Lessee responsible for servicing and maintenance
- Primary period of lease for asset's useful economic life, secondary (low-rent) period afterwards
- Asset shown on lessee's balance sheet

Advantages of leasing

- ☑ Supplier paid in full
- ☑ Lessor receives (taxable) income and capital allowances
- ☑ Help lessee's cash flow
- ☑ Cheaper than bank loan?

Sale and leaseback

is when a business agrees to sell one of its assets to a financial institution and leases it back.

Steps in lease or buy decision for tax-paying organisation

1 Make acquisition decision using present value of costs and benefits, assuming asset is purchased for cash in year 0

Use after-tax investment cost of capital (WACC)

2 Make financing decision (lease or buy) using only present value of cash flows affected by financing decision

Use after-tax cost of borrowing

Finance leases and tax

Tax rules may allow:

- Depreciation as expense
- Interest element as expense

The assumption may be that lease payments are allowable for tax in full.

Other considerations

- Running expenses
- Liquidity
- Alternative uses of funds
- Uncertainty over trade-in value

9: The cost of capital

Topic List

An exam question may ask you to explain the assumptions behind the weighted average cost of capital, or what happens to the cost of capital and financial risk if gearing changes.

Elements of cost of capital

Risk free rate of return	Return required from a completely risk free investment eg yield on government securities
Business risk premium	Increase in required rate of return due to uncertainty about future and business prospects
Financial risk premium	Danger of high debt levels, variability of equity returns

Private companies

No market values available.

- Use cost of capital for similar public companies, adding premiums for business and financial risk

- Take risk-free rate of return and add premiums for business and financial risk

Marginal cost of capital approach

- Establish rates of return for each component of capital structure
- Relate dividends/interest to these values
- Apply marginal cost to each component depending on its proportionate weight

Cost of capital if constant dividends paid

$$k_e = \frac{d}{P_0} \qquad \text{Exam formula}$$

where P_0 is price at time
  d is dividend
  k_e is cost of equity or preference capital

Dividend growth model

$$k_e = \frac{d_0(1+g)}{P_0} + g = \frac{d_1}{P_0} + g \qquad \text{Exam formula}$$

where d_0 is dividend at time 0
  d_1 is dividend at time 1
  g is dividend growth rate

Estimating growth rate

Use experience or formula (Gordon's growth model)

$$g = bR$$

where R is accounting return on capital employed
  b is proportion of earnings retained

$$g = \sqrt[n]{\frac{\text{dividend in year x}}{\text{dividend in year x} - n}} - 1$$

9: The cost of capital

After tax cost of irredeemable debt capital

$$k_{dnet} = \frac{i\,(1-t)}{P_0} \qquad \textbf{Exam formula}$$

where k_{dnet} is the after-tax cost of the debt capital

i is the annual interest payment

P_0 is the current market price of the debt capital ex-interest

t is the rate of tax

Cost of redeemable securities

$$P_0 = \frac{i}{(1+k_{dnet})} + \frac{i}{(1+k_{dnet})^2} + \ldots + \frac{i+P_n}{(1+k_{dnet})^n}$$

where P_n is amount payable on redemption in year n

This equation has to be solved using different discount factors to find the IRR.

Year	Item	Cash	DCF	PV
0	Current Market value	(X)	1.000	(X)
1–n	Interest less tax ($i\,(1-t)$)	X	X	X
n	Value of shares on conversion	X	X	X
				X

Assumptions of WACC

- Project small relative to company and has same business risk as company
- WACC reflects company's long-term future capital structure and costs
- New investments financed by new funds
- Cost of capital reflects marginal cost

Problems with WACC

- New investments may have different business risk
- New finance may change capital structure and perceived financial risk
- Cost of floating rate capital not easy to calculate

$$WACC = k_e \frac{V_E}{V_E+V_D} + k_d \frac{V_D}{V_E+V_D}$$ **Exam formula**

k_e is cost of equity
k_d is cost of debt

V_E is market value of equity
V_D is market value of debt

Use market values rather than book values unless market values unavailable (unquoted company)

Assumptions

- All earnings paid out as dividends
- Earnings and business risk constant
- No issue costs
- Tax ignored

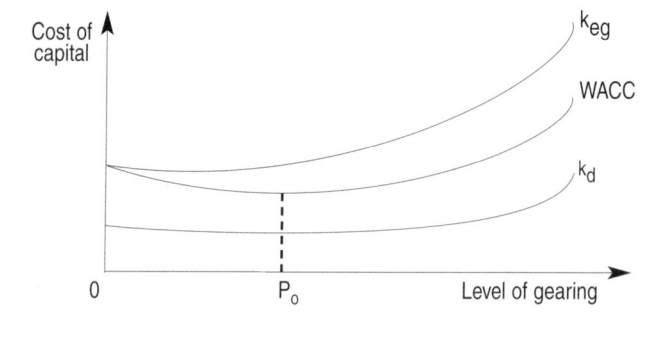

k_{eg}	is the cost of equity in the geared company
k_d	is the cost of debt
WACC	is the weighted average cost of capital
P_0	is the optimal capital structure where WACC is lowest

Modigliani and Miller concluded that the capital structure of a company would have no effect on the overall Weighted Average Cost of Capital.

Assumptions made by M&M

- Investors are rational

- Information is freely available

- No transaction costs

- Debt is risk-free

- Investors are indifferent between corporate and personal borrowing

M&M argued that cost of equity would rise as gearing rises to offset exactly the benefits of the increasing proportion of lower-cost debt capital.

Arbitrage

M&M assume that arbitrage by investors (buying and selling securities to profit from different market prices) would keep WACC constant.

Problems with M&M

- Investors risk differs between personal/corporate gearing

- Individual's cost of borrowing is higher

- Transaction costs restrict arbitrage

- Can't identify identical firms

- Some earnings will be retained

9: The cost of capital

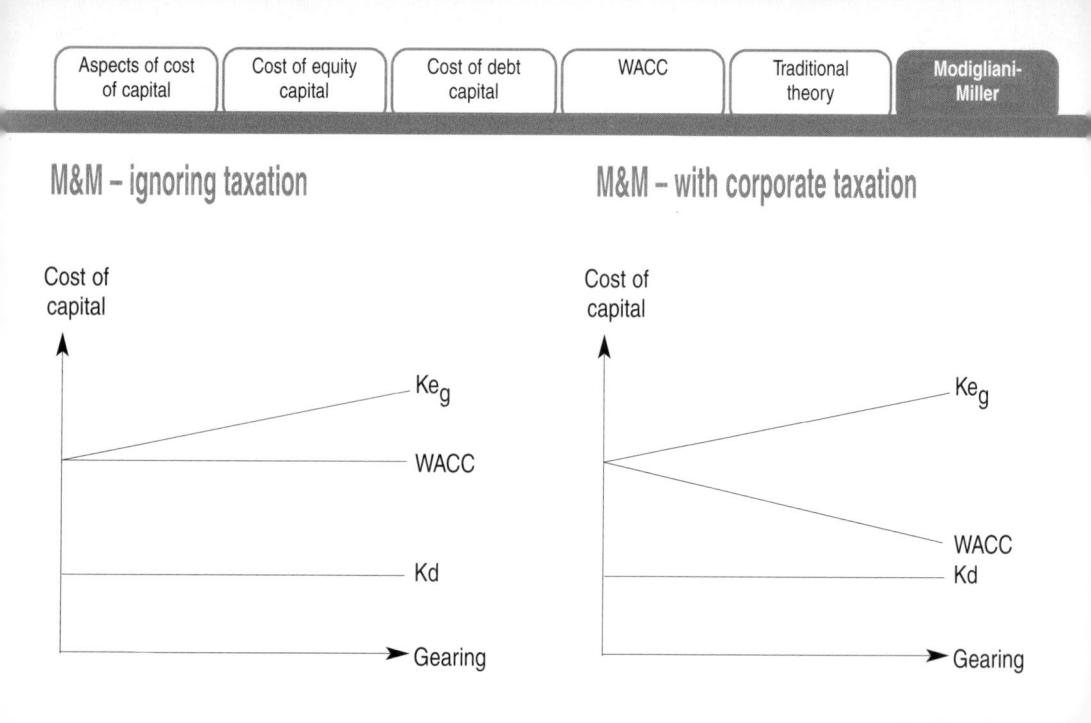

M&M – ignoring taxation

Cost of capital

Ke_g

WACC

Kd

Gearing

M&M – with corporate taxation

Cost of capital

Ke_g

WACC
Kd

Gearing

Impact of tax

- Tax relief on interest payments lowers WACC, and WACC continues to fall up to very high gearing levels

- Equilibrium level of debt for economy depends on rate of company tax, personal tax and funds available. At this point effect of tax shield for companies equals interest levels for investors

M & M cost of equity formula allowing for taxes

$$k_{eg} = k_{eu} + \left[k_{eu} - k_d \right] \frac{V_D (1 - t)}{V_E}$$

Exam formula

k_{eg}	is cost of equity of a geared company
k_{eu}	is cost of equity / WACC of a similar ungeared company
V_D	is market value of debt capital in the geared company
V_E	is market value of equity in the geared company
t	is tax rate

M&M WACC/Adjusted cost of capital

$$r^* = r\,(1 - T^*L) \qquad \text{Exam formula}$$

where r^* is WACC of geared company
  r is WACC of ungeared company
  T^* is tax saving on interest (decimal)

  L is equivalent to $\dfrac{V_D}{V_D + V_E}$

$$\text{Or } k_{adj} = k_{eu}\,(1 - tL) \qquad \text{Exam formula}$$

This can be used in investment appraisal to reflect financing side-effects.

M&M WACC formula

$$V_g = V_u + TB_C \qquad \text{Exam formula}$$

where V_u is value of ungeared company
  V_g is value of geared company
  TB_C is total tax benefit

TB_C is tax shield on debt, the amount by which value of geared company exceeds value of ungeared company.

10: The capital structure decision

Topic List

Determining capital structure

Working capital management

This chapter summarises the key factors that will determine the mix of equity and debt finance an organisation uses. You need to be able to discuss what factors are particularly important in determining capital structure, and how restrictions on financing may influence an organisation's strategy.

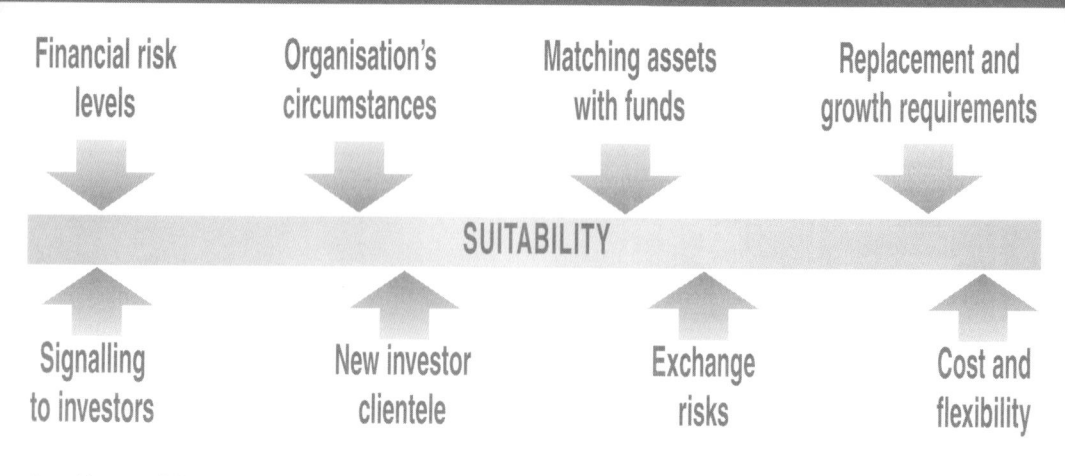

Consider possibility of optimum gearing level at which cost of capital is minimised. Consider also effect on earnings and dividends of more gearing.

Attitudes to risk	Loss of control	Acceptable interest burden	Level of commitments	Availability of current sources

ACCEPTABILITY

FEASIBILITY

Attitudes of lenders	Availability of equity	Future availability	Restrictions in loan agreements	Loan maturity

10: The capital structure decision

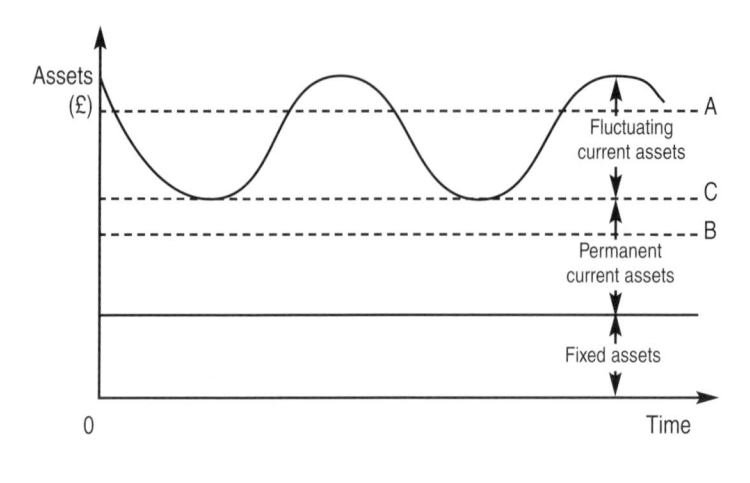

In A (conservative) all permanent and some fluctuating current assets financed out of long-term sources; may be surplus cash for investment.

In B (aggressive) all fluctuating and some permanent current assets financed out of short-term sources, possible liquidity problems.

In C long-term funds finance permanent assets, short-term funds non-permanent assets.

11: Portfolios and diversification

You need to have a basic understanding of the principles behind diversification and the importance of the market portfolio.

Positive correlation

If one investment does well, other will also do well.

Negative correlation

If one investment does well, other will do badly.

No correlation

Performance of one investment will be independent of other.

For the same expected return, the risk (standard deviation)

- Is highest for perfect positive correlation between individual securities in portfolio
- Is lower when there is no correlation
- Is lowest when there is perfect negative correlation

Investors choose a portfolio which balances

- Expected returns
- Risk that actual returns of portfolio will vary from expected returns
- Security
- Liquidity

Diversification by companies

Advantages	Disadvantages
☑ Internal cash flows less volatile	☒ Best opportunities in familiar markets
☑ International diversification reduces systematic risk	☒ Diversify away from skills/knowledge possessed
☑ Lower probability of corporate failure	☒ Vulnerable to unbundling takeovers
In particular investors can probably reduce investment risk better than companies.	

Limitations of portfolio analysis

- Estimating probabilities of different outcomes
- Establishing shareholders' preference
- Not in manager's own interests

- Not easy to divide holdings
- Constant returns to scale assumed
- Doesn't cover all aspects of risk

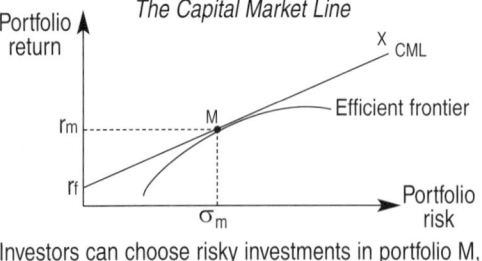

The Capital Market Line

Investors can choose risky investments in portfolio M, or risk free investments with return r_f

Risk premium

Risk premium is the risk investor requires as compensation for accepting portfolio risk.

$$\text{Risk premium} = \frac{\sigma_p}{\sigma_m}(R_m - R_f)$$

where

R_f is risk-free rate of return

R_m is return on market portfolio, M

σ_m is risk of returns in portfolio M

σ_p is risk of returns in portfolio P

$\frac{\sigma_p}{\sigma_m}$ represents the beta factor β, the extent to which a portfolio's return should exceed risk-free rate

12: The capital asset pricing model

Topic List

The CAPM formula is one of the most important in this paper and you need to feel comfortable using it and recognising all its elements when they are supplied in questions.

Gearing betas is one of the most demanding topics in this paper, but you can make life easier by following the step approach that we have outlined.

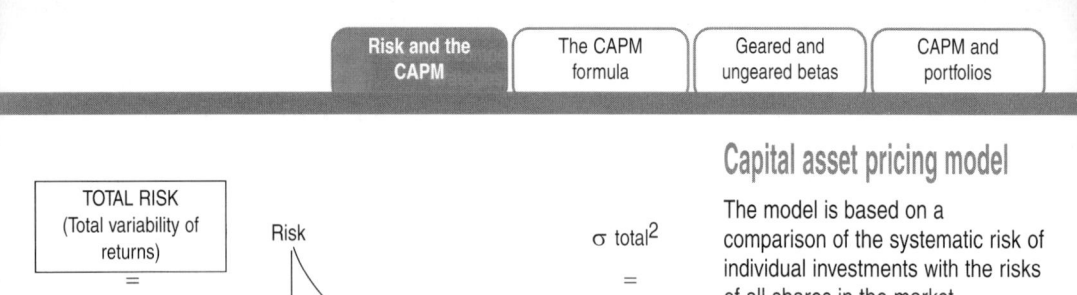

Capital asset pricing model

The model is based on a comparison of the systematic risk of individual investments with the risks of all shares in the market.

Assumes:

- Investors/Companies require return in excess of risk-free rate

- Unsystematic risk can be diversified away and no premium is required for it

- Investors/Companies require a higher return from investments where systematic risk is greater

Model tries to establish share's equilibrium value/cost of equity

The CAPM formula

$$k_e = R_f + (R_m - R_f)\,\beta \qquad \text{Exam formula}$$

where k_e is cost of equity capital/expected equity return

R_f is risk-free rate of return

R_m is return from market

β is beta factor of security

Market risk premium

is the extra return required from a share to compensate for its risk compared with average market risk.

Problems with CAPM

Assumptions unrealistic?

- Zero insolvency costs
- Investment market efficient
- Investors hold well-diversified portfolios
- Perfect capital market

Required estimates difficult to make

- Excess return
- Risk-free rate (govt. securities' rates vary with lending terms)
- β factors difficult to calculate

12: The capital asset pricing model

$$\beta_u = \beta_g \frac{V_E}{V_E + V_D(1-t)} + \beta_d \frac{V_D(1-t)}{V_E + V_D(1-t)}$$ **Exam formula**

Where β_u is beta factor of ungeared company; ungeared beta

β_g is beta factor in similar but geared company; geared beta

β_d is beta factor of debt in geared company

V_D is market value of debt capital in geared company

V_E is market value of equity in geared company

t is rate of corporate tax

Debt is often assumed to be risk-free and β_d part of equation thus would equal 0.

Beta factors can also be estimated by using Beta values of other quoted companies with similar characteristics. However:

- Difficult to identify firms with identical characteristics
- Estimates of beta values from share price information may not be accurate
- Differences in beta values between firms caused by cost structures, size, and growth opportunities

CAPM can be used to find discount rate for project involving diversification into new business, and which thus will have different systematic risk level.

Step 1. Estimate systematic risk characteristics of project's operating cash flows by obtaining published beta values for companies in same industry as company undertaking project.

Step 2. Adjust beta values of other companies in industry to reflect company's capital structure.

(a) Convert beta values of geared companies in industry to ungeared betas using

$$\beta_u = \frac{\beta_g}{\left[1 + \frac{V_D(1-t)}{V_E}\right]}$$

(b) Convert ungeared beta back to geared beta that reflects company's own gearing ratio using

$$\beta_g = \beta_u\left[1 + \frac{V_D(1-t)}{V_E}\right]$$

Step 3. Use CAPM to estimate project specific cost of equity, and use cost of equity and company's cost of debt capital to estimate WACC.

Beta factor of portfolios

- Portfolio consisting of all securities on stock market (excluding risk-free) will have Beta factor of 1

- Portfolio consisting entirely of risk-free securities will have Beta factor of 0

- Beta factor of investor's portfolio is weighted average of Beta factors of securities in portfolio

Implications of CAPM for investors

- Decide on desired Beta factors

- Invest in low β shares when returns falling (bear)

- Invest in high β shares when returns rising (bull)

Arbitrage pricing theory

The theory assumes that the return on each security is based on a number of independent factors.

$$r = E(r_j) + B_1 F_1 + B_2 F_2 \ldots + e$$

Where
$E(r_j)$ is expected return on security

B_1 is sensitivity to changes in Factor 1

F_1 is difference between Factor 1 actual and expected values

B_2 is sensitivity to changes in Factor 2

F_2 is difference between Factor 2 actual...

e is a random term

Main problem – identifying macroeconomic factors and risk sensitivities.

Topic List

The finance function

Scope of treasury function

Centralising treasury function

Cost or profit centre

You need to be aware of the scope of the work of the finance and treasury functions. A written question may ask you to compare what each does.

Alternatively, it may ask you about the main decisions that need to be made in relation to each function. Should the finance function be outsourced? Should the treasury function be a cost or profit centre?

Responsibilities of finance function

- Preparation and monitoring of budgets
- Preparation of monthly, quarterly and annual accounts
- Preparation of other relevant information
- Management of payroll and internal audit
- Managing relationships with stakeholders

Assessment of finance function

- Provision of reliable data
- Technically up to date
- Speed of data provision
- Efficiency
- Balanced scorecard

Stakeholder relationships

- **Internal** - relevant information for those who need it
- **Business advisers** - information required for advice
- **Auditors** - external/internal audit links
- **Investors** - results and financial management
- **Financiers** - details of profits and liquidity

Balanced scorecard

- Value enhancements
- Customer satisfaction
- Improved internal processes
- Learning and growth
- Benchmarking

Business partner

Business partner model has been developed in response to criticisms that finance function too concerned with control and past performance. Gives finance function a more active role in providing information, and explains its role to cover strategic issues such as investment.

Outsourcing

Outsourcing of basic transaction processing and payroll management is now common, with finance function concentrating on provision of key information. Alternative is use of shared service centres.

Problems with business partner model

- Loss of independence
- Too identified with operational managers
- Failure to provide sufficient control
- Lack of focus on providing true and fair view external stakeholders require

Independent business partner

Finance function's role to add value not create it. Focus should be safeguarding of assets and effective reporting, also rigorous assessment and validation of strategic ideas.

Treasury management is the corporate handling of all financial matters, the generation of funds for business, the management of currencies and cash flows and the strategies, policies and procedures of corporate finance.

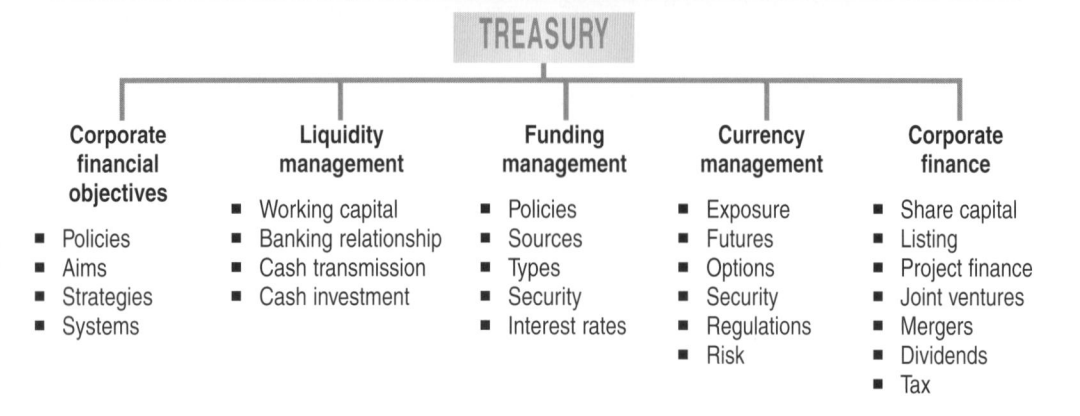

TREASURY

Corporate financial objectives

- Policies
- Aims
- Strategies
- Systems

Liquidity management

- Working capital
- Banking relationship
- Cash transmission
- Cash investment

Funding management

- Policies
- Sources
- Types
- Security
- Interest rates

Currency management

- Exposure
- Futures
- Options
- Security
- Regulations
- Risk

Corporate finance

- Share capital
- Listing
- Project finance
- Joint ventures
- Mergers
- Dividends
- Tax

If a company has a large number of subsidiaries or divisions, does it centralise treasury functions (and have central department acting as group banker) or allow each subsidiary to carry out its own treasury functions?

Centralised treasury management

- ☑ Avoids surplus/deficits mix
- ☑ Bulk cash flows and lower bank charges
- ☑ More short-term investment opportunities
- ☑ Foreign currency risk decreased by matching
- ☑ Employ experts
- ☑ Smaller total precautionary balance
- ☑ Can be profit centre focusing on efficiency and cost minimisation
- ☑ Better control framework
- ☑ Common technology

Decentralised treasury management

- ☑ Diversified finance sources match local assets
- ☑ Greater autonomy for subsidiaries and divisions
- ☑ More responsive to local needs esp worldwide

Outsourcing

Outsourcing or shared service centres may be most economic way of obtaining expertise, but consider needs of business.

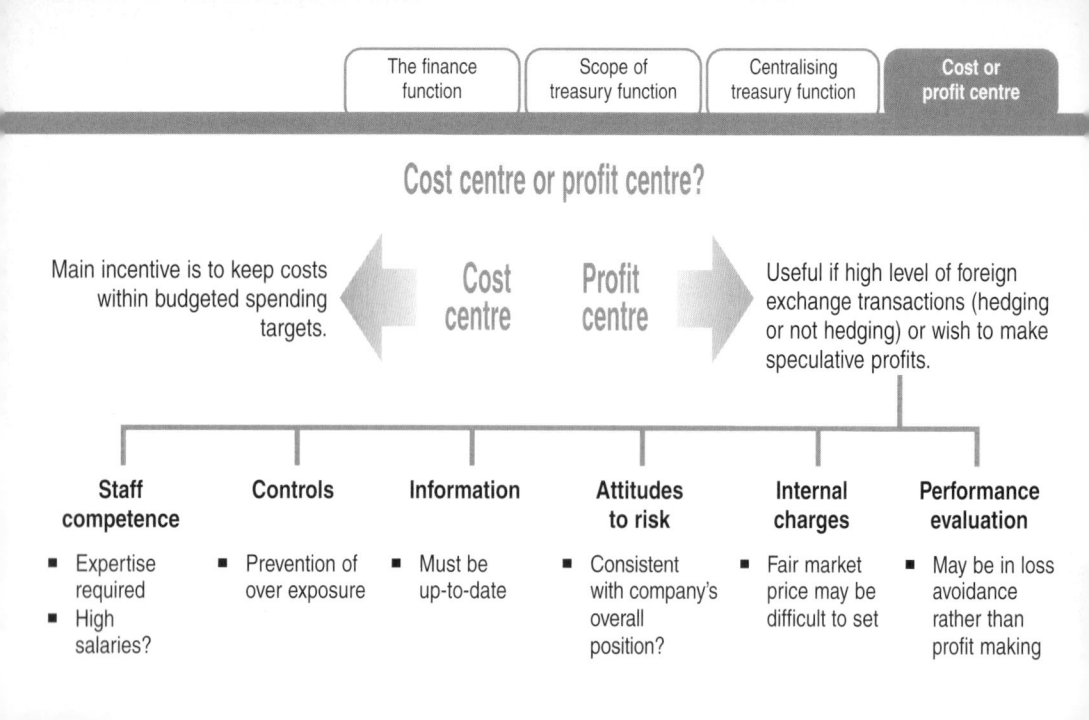

Cost centre or profit centre?

Cost centre ← Main incentive is to keep costs within budgeted spending targets.

Profit centre → Useful if high level of foreign exchange transactions (hedging or not hedging) or wish to make speculative profits.

Staff competence
- Expertise required
- High salaries?

Controls
- Prevention of over exposure

Information
- Must be up-to-date

Attitudes to risk
- Consistent with company's overall position?

Internal charges
- Fair market price may be difficult to set

Performance evaluation
- May be in loss avoidance rather than profit making

15: Valuation techniques

Topic List

Asset valuation

Earnings valuation

Dividend valuation

Cash flow valuation

Other bases

Intellectual capital

The topics in this chapter may well be examined as part of a compulsory question on a takeover situation, where you have to value a company by various methods.

You should also consider the degree of market efficiency. How much information does the market have? How good is it at anticipating mergers?

Net assets valuation method

Value of shares in class $=$ $\dfrac{\text{Net assets attributable to class}}{\text{No of shares in class}}$

Possible bases of valuation

Historic basis
(unlikely to be realistic)

Replacement basis
(asset used on ongoing basis)

Realisable basis
(asset sold/ business broken up)

Uses of net asset valuation method

- As measure of security in a share valuation

- As measure of comparison in scheme of merger

- As floor value in business that is up for sale

Problems in valuation

- Need for professional valuation

- Realisation of assets

- Contingent liabilities

- Market for assets

Price - earnings ratio

$$\text{P/E ratio} = \frac{\text{Market value}}{\text{EPS}}$$

$$\text{Market value} = \text{EPS} \times \text{P/E ratio}$$

Have to decide suitable P/E ratio.

Factors to consider:

- Industry
- Status
- Marketability
- Shareholders
- Asset backing and liquidity
- Nature of assets
- Gearing

Accounting rate of return

$$\text{Value of business} = \frac{\text{Estimated future profits}}{\text{Required return on capital employed}}$$

In a takeover bid, there may be adjustments required for new levels of directors' remuneration, interest charges and rationalisation. ARR is used to decide maximum amount to pay in a takeover.

Earnings yield valuation model

$$\text{Market value} = \frac{\text{Earnings}}{\text{Earnings yield}}$$

15: Valuation techniques

Dividend valuation model

$$P_0 = \frac{d}{k_e}$$

Where P_0 is price at time 0

d is Dividend (constant)

k_e is cost of equity

$$P_0 = \frac{d_1}{k_e - g}$$ **Exam formula**

Where d_1 is dividend in year 1

g is dividend growth rate

Assumptions

- Dividends from new projects of same risk type as existing operations
- No increase in cost of capital
- Perfect information
- Shareholders have same marginal capital cost
- Ignore tax and issue expenses

Problems

- Companies that don't pay dividends don't have zero values
- Need enough profitable projects to maintain dividends
- Dividend policy likely to change on takeover

Discounted cash flows method

> Value investment using expected after-tax cash flows of investment and appropriate cost of capital.

Free cash flow

> Value of company is sum of future free cash flows.
>
> Revenues
> - Operating costs
> + Depreciation
> + Interest (1 – tax rate)
> - Taxes
> - Debt repayment
> - Working capital
> - Investment expenditure

Shareholder value analysis

Analysis focuses on key decisions affecting value and risk. Decisions depend on value drivers (eg profit margin, working capital, required return).

Problems with cash flow methods

- Difficult to select appropriate cost of capital
- Unreliable estimates of future cash flows
- Not best method for minority interests who lack influence on cash flows

Super-profits method of valuation

Step 1. Apply fair return to net tangible assets

Step 2. Compare result with expected profits

Step 3. Use excess of expected profits over fair profits (super-profits) to calculate goodwill (super-profits × x years)

Step 4. Add goodwill to value of tangible assets to arrive at business value

The main problems are that the rate of return and number of years are chosen subjectively.

Earn-out arrangements

are where buyer of business agrees to pay seller an additional amount of consideration if acquired company achieves a certain performance level.

It is only appropriate to use the method if the acquired company is to be run independently of the buyer's company for the period upon which the contingent consideration is based.

Buyers have to use probability analysis to assess best, worst and most likely outcomes.

> **Intellectual capital is knowledge that can be used to create value.**

Human resources

- Skills
- Experience
- Knowledge

Intellectual assets

- Drawing
- Computer program
- Data collection

Intellectual property

Legally protected assets

- Patents
- Copyrights

Market-to-book values

Value of firm's intellectual capital
= Market value of firm − Intangible assets book value

Tobin's q

Market capitalisation   : Replacement cost
(share price × no of shares)   of assets

Calculated intangible value

Calculates market value of intangible assets on the basis of company's return on tangible assets over industry's average return on tangible assets.

Relief from royalties method

Determination of revenue (licensing revenues, royalties savings), application of notional royalty rate to produce royalty stream which is capitalised and discounted at risk-free rate.

Types of intangible assets

- Patents, trademarks and copyrights
- Franchises and licensing agreements
- Research and development
- Brands
- Technology
- Know-how
- Customer loyalty
- Distribution channels

Premium profits method

Valuation based on extra profits generated by brand/other intangible (shown by difference in price). Also important for brands are market durability, advertising support, competition.

Capitalisation of earnings method

Estimate maintainable earnings and apply earnings multiple taking account of future prospects and risks.

Comparison with market transactions method

Valuations on basis of market transactions in similar assets.

16: Amalgamations and restructuring

All the topics in this chapter are important . Questions on mergers and acquisitions are likely to be set as compulsory questions, and be wide-ranging, with both calculations and comments required.

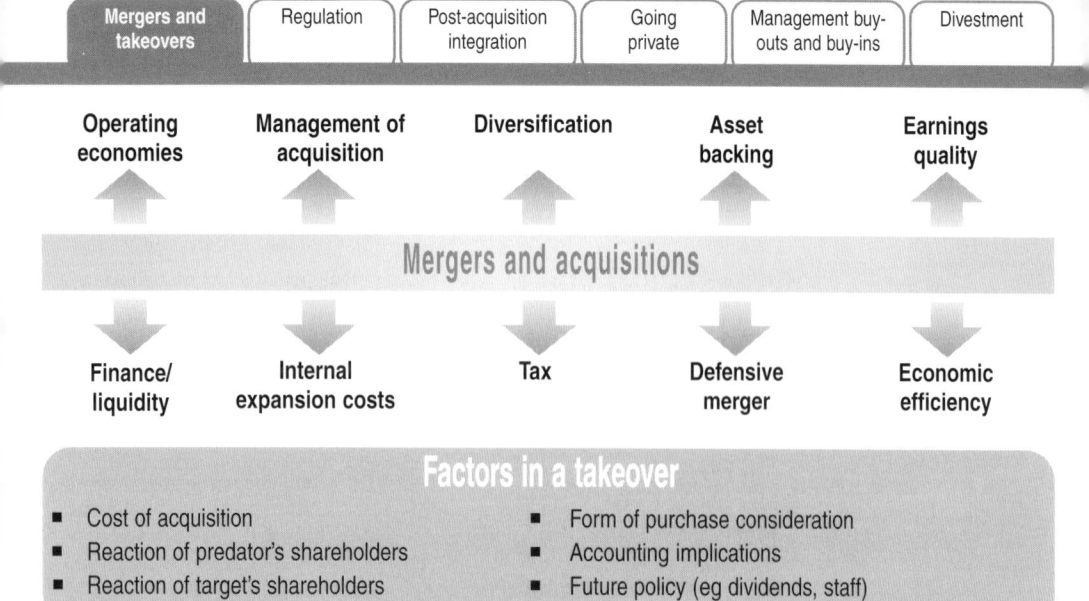

| Mergers and takeovers | Regulation | Post-acquisition integration | Going private | Management buy-outs and buy-ins | Divestment |

Operating economies · **Management of acquisition** · **Diversification** · **Asset backing** · **Earnings quality**

Mergers and acquisitions

Finance/liquidity · **Internal expansion costs** · **Tax** · **Defensive merger** · **Economic efficiency**

Factors in a takeover

- Cost of acquisition
- Reaction of predator's shareholders
- Reaction of target's shareholders

- Form of purchase consideration
- Accounting implications
- Future policy (eg dividends, staff)

TAKEOVER STRATEGY

ACQUIRE

Growth prospects limited → Younger company with higher growth rate

Potential to sell other products to existing customers → Company with complementary product range

Operating at maximum capacity → Company making similar products operating below capacity

Under-utilising management → Company needing better management

Greater control over supplies or customers → Company giving access to customer/supplier

Lacking key clients in targeted sector → Company with right customer profile

Improve balance sheet → Company enhancing EPS

Increase market share → Important competitor

Widen capability → Key talents and/or technology

Approval of predator's shareholders

Approval may be required under Stock Exchange rules, or because market price of shares will fall if shareholders are unhappy with the value of the takeover.

Possible objections

- Reduction in EPS
- Target in risky industry
- Target facing liquidation
- Reduction in overall net asset backing

Resistance by target company

- Unwillingness to sell
- Cash offer not satisfactory
- Shares offered in exchange being unattractive
- No post-acquisition advantages
- Opposition of employees

Defensive tactics

- Persuading shareholders offer is poor
- Advertising campaign
- White knight/poison-pill
- Counterbid for predator
- Management buy-out

Purchase consideration

Cash purchases　　　**Share exchange**　　　**Convertible loan stock**

Choice of offer

Predator's shareholders

- EPS dilution
- Tax allowable interest
- Change in gearing
- Change in effective control

Target's shareholders

- Liability to tax on cash capital gain
- Maintain existing income
- Maintain stake in company
- Want shares to retain value

If cash consideration is used, cash may have to be raised by rights issues or borrowing (medium-term loans or mezzanine finance).

If the takeover is to be by a share exchange, it may fail if predator's shares fall in value or target's rise.

Effect on EPS

If target company's shares are bought at a higher P/E ratio than predator's shares, then predator company's shareholders will suffer a fall in EPS.

If target company's shares are valued at lower P/E ratio, predator company's shares will benefit from rise in EPS.

A dilution of earnings on an acquisition may be accepted in certain circumstances, such as earnings growth, superior quality of target's earnings, or increase in asset backing.

A single dividend policy will also be needed, that will satisfy both sets of shareholders.

Valuation using post-merger flows

Use as basis dividends or cash flows of merged company.

- Estimate initial dividends of combined company + dividend growth rate
- Estimate new cost of capital
- Calculate value of combined company
- Compare with value of acquiror: excess is value of target

City Code

is a UK code which companies are expected to follow during a takeover or merger. Administered by UK's Takeover Panel. An example of good practice.

General principles

- All offeree's shareholders treated similarly
- Information available to all shareholders
- Shareholders given sufficient information/advice
- Shareholders given time to make decision
- Directors not to frustrate takeover
- No oppression of minorities
- Offer to all shareholders when control (30%) acquired

Competition authorities

Competition authorities may act against mergers not felt to be in the public interest, by rejecting them outright or laying down conditions.

European rules
Act against competition restrictions in EU
If Commission finds mergers incompatible with common market, can prevent them

Drucker's rules for acquiror

- Need for common core of unity
- Ask what can offer acquired company
- Treat products, markets and customers of acquired company with respect
- Provide top management with relevant skills for acquired company
- Cross-company promotions of staff

Jones' integration sequence

Step 1. Communicate initial reporting relationships

Step 2. Acquire rapid control of key factors

Step 3. Resource audit

Step 4. Re-define corporate objectives

Step 5. Revise organisational structure

Failure of mergers and takeovers

- Poor strategic plan
- Over-optimism
- Inflexibility of integration methods
- Poor man management
- Cultural differences
- Lack of knowledge of target
- Poor management in target

Research shows that financial institutions, target company shareholders and the acquiring company management tend to benefit most.

Going private

occurs when a small group of individuals, possibly including existing shareholders and management, buy all the company's shares. The company ceases to be listed on a stock exchange and shares may thus lose some value.

Spin-off

is when a new company is created whose shares are owned by the shareholders of the original company. There is no change in asset ownership, but management may change.

Advantages of going private to company

- Costs of meeting listing requirements can be saved
- Company protected from volatility in share prices which may create financial problems
- Company less vulnerable to hostile takeover bids
- Management can concentrate on long-term business

Advantages of spin-offs to investors

- Merger or takeover of only part of business made easier
- Improved efficiency/management
- Easier to see value of separate parts
- Investors can adjust shareholdings

Management buy-outs (MBOs)

is the purchase of all or part of a business by its managers. The managers generally need financial backers (venture capital) who will want an equity stake).

Reasons for company agreeing to MBO are similar to those for sell-off, also:

- Best offer price available is from MBO
- When group has decided to sell subsidiary, best way of maximising management co-operation
- Sale can be arranged quickly
- Selling organisation more likely to retain beneficial links with sold segment

Evaluation of MBOs by investors

- Management skills of team
- Reasons why company is being sold
- Projected profits, cash flows and risks
- Shares/selected assets being bought
- Price right?
- Financial contribution by management team
- Exit routes (flotation, share repurchase)

Venture capital

Venture capitalists are often prepared to fund MBOs. They require shareholding, right to appoint some directors and right of veto on certain business decisions.

Performance of MBOs

Generally better than previous situation. Reasons:

- Favourable price
- Personal motivation
- Quicker decision - making/flexibility
- Savings on overheads

Buy-ins

are when a team of outside managers mount a takeover bid and then run the business themselves.

Problems with MBOs

- Lack of financial experience
- Tax and legal complications
- Changing work practices
- Inadequate cash flow
- Board representation by finance suppliers
- Loss of employees/suppliers/customers

Buy-ins often occur when a business is in trouble or shareholder/managers wish to retire. Finance sources are similar to buy-outs. They work best if management quality improves, but external managers may face opposition from employees.

A divestment is a proportionate or complete reduction in ownership stake in an organisation.

Demerger

is the splitting up of a corporate body into two or more separate bodies, to ensure share prices reflect the true value of underlying operations.

Sell-off

is the sale of part of a company to a third party, generally for cash.

Disadvantages of demergers

- Loss of economies of scale
- Ability to raise extra finance reduced
- Vulnerability to takeover increased

Reasons for sell-offs

- Strategic restructuring
- Sell off loss-making part
- Protect rest of business from takeover
- Cash shortage
- Reduction of business risk
- Sale at profit

17: Elements of investment appraisal

Topic List

Relevant costs

Benefits and risks

Design of products and services

IT investment

Foreign investment

Transfer pricing

Before we cover the 'numbers' element of investment appraisal, this chapter covers wider issues that may need to be brought into the discussion parts of appraisal questions. Be warned however that being able to identify relevant costs and benefits is important, and will affect appraisal calculations.

Many investments you see will be international investments, as in the May 2005 exam.

Opportunity costs

Costs incurred or **revenues** lost from diverting **existing resources** from their best use.

Example

Costs of diverting a salesman to new project from existing activities, will be income he would have generated from existing activities and *not* his salary, which would be paid whatever he's involved with.

Finance cash flows

Ignore dividends; interest only relevant if project financed at special rate $\neq$ WACC.

Tax

Tax considerations include tax on profits (or losses), also tax effect of tax allowable depreciation.

Other costs

- Working capital (see Chapter 18)
- Infrastructure
- Market, eg research, promotion and branding
- Human resource, eg training and reorganisation

Benefits

- Savings in staff and other operating costs
- Additional sales contribution
- More efficient systems
- Revenue from sales of old assets

Intangible benefits

- Quicker service to customers
- Greater customer satisfaction
- Greater staff satisfaction
- Management and control improvements

Risks

- **Physical** - Fire, computer failure
- **Economic** - Adverse conditions
- **Financial** - Source problems
- **Business** - New technology, competitor and customer reaction
- **Political** - Instability, sanctions
- **Exchange** - Adverse movements
- **Information** - Unreliable data

Dealing with risk

Consider in context of acceptable risks for investment/overall portfolio.

Measure **uncertainty** by operational research.

Measure risk using, eg expected values and deal with critical variables.

17: Elements of investment appraisal

Reasons for new product development

- Changing needs of customers (adequate demand)
- Competitive advantage
- Environmental threats and opportunities
- Extend/refresh the product portfolio
- Extend product life

Services

As services are intangible, cannot be stored and vary with each delivery. Consider:

- Location of operations
- Premises layout and environment
- Whether demands can be smoothed
- Quality standards
- Time standards
- Length of forecasts

Stages of new development

Initial assessment

▼

Business analysis

▼

Product design

▼

Early testing

▼

Final testing

▼

Product launch

IT investment must link in with a business's strategic, operational and control needs, and be based on strong **business case** analysis.

Relevant costs of IT

- **Hardware** - computers, peripherals
- **Installation** - new buildings, furniture
- **Development** - analysis, design, changeover costs
- **Personnel** - staff training, new staff
- **Operating** - consumables, maintenance, accommodation, standby
- **Intangible** - learning curve, incompatibility of current systems

Direct benefits of IT

- Savings of costs of old systems
- Efficiency savings
- Operational savings
- Increased sales revenues

Indirect benefits of IT

- Improved staff morale
- Less time on routine tasks
- Better planning/decision-making
- Better customer service

17: Elements of investment appraisal

Backwards integration – acquisition of raw material or component sources overseas

Foreign direct investment ➡ **Diversification**

Forward integration – establishing final production and distribution outlets overseas

Means

- New start-up investments
- Overseas takeover/merger means of acquiring market share and distribution channels
- Joint ventures

Alternatives

- Exporting directly, or through agents
- Licensing, giving overseas producers rights to production process in return for royalties
- **Countertrade** - non arms-length transaction, including barter, counterpurchase and purchaser involvement in production (offset)

A joint venture is a project undertaken by two or more persons/entities joining together with a view to profit, often in connection with a single operation.

Contractual joint venture

is for a fixed period, and duties and responsibilities of parties are contractually defined.

Joint-equity venture

involves investment, is of no fixed duration, and continually evolves.

Reasons for establishing subsidiaries

- **Location of markets** - save shipping costs if manufacture overseas
- **Sales organisation** - sales team with local knowledge
- **Lower costs** - labour is cheaper or access to raw materials is easier
- **Import controls** - overseas presence can mean import controls/tariffs are avoided.

Need to consider method of funding, gearing and profit retention of subsidiary

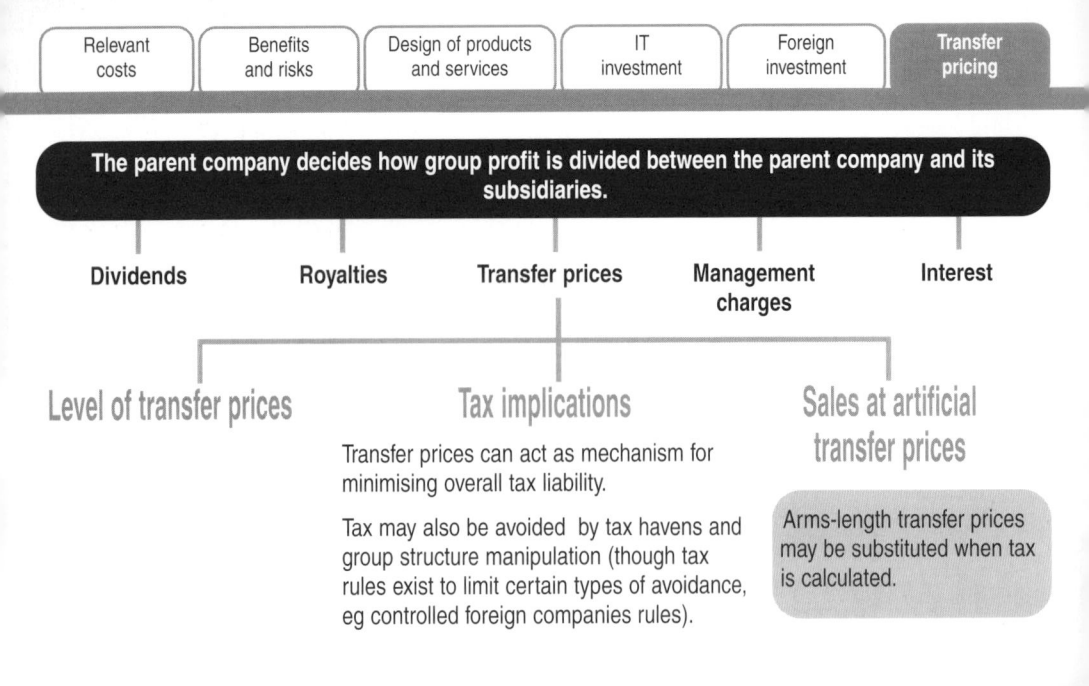

The parent company decides how group profit is divided between the parent company and its subsidiaries.

| Dividends | Royalties | Transfer prices | Management charges | Interest |

Level of transfer prices

Tax implications

Transfer prices can act as mechanism for minimising overall tax liability.

Tax may also be avoided by tax havens and group structure manipulation (though tax rules exist to limit certain types of avoidance, eg controlled foreign companies rules).

Sales at artificial transfer prices

Arms-length transfer prices may be substituted when tax is calculated.

18: Investment appraisal methods

Topic List

Payback

Accounting rate of return

NPV and IRR

Inflation

Taxation

International investment appraisal

Any investment appraisal question at this level will feature a number of complications, so be aware of how inflation and taxation may affect calculations. You may be asked to carry out an investment appraisal in sterling or another currency.

Payback

is the time taken for the cash inflows from a capital investment project to equal the cash outflows, usually expressed in years.

It is used as a minimum target/first screening method.

Example

£'000	P	Q
Investment	60	60
Yr 1 profits	20	50
Yr 2 profits	30	20
Yr 3 profits	50	5

Q pays back first, but ultimately P's profits are higher on the same amount of investment.

Advantages

☑ Simple to calculate and understand
☑ Concentrates on short-term, less risky flows
☑ Can identify quick cash generators

Disadvantages

☒ Ignores timing of flows after payback period
☒ Ignores total project return
☒ Ignores time value of money
☒ Arbitrary choice of cut-off

Accounting rate of return

- Also known as return on capital employed or return on investment.

- Can be used to rank projects taking place over a number of years (using average profits and investment).

- Can also rank mutually exclusive projects.

Method of calculation

$$\frac{\text{Estimated average profits}}{\text{Estimated average investment}} \times 100\%$$

Advantages	Disadvantages
☑ Quick and simple calculation	☒ Takes no account of timing
☑ Easy to understand % return	☒ Based on accounting profits, not cash flows
☑ Looks at entire project life	☒ Relative, not absolute, measure
	☒ Ignores time value of money
	☒ Takes no account of project length

Net present value (NPV)

is the value obtained by discounting all cash flows of project by target rate of return/cost of capital. If NPV is positive, the project will be accepted, if negative it will be rejected.

Features of NPV

- Uses all cash flows related to project
- Allows timing of cash flows
- Can be calculated using generally accepted method

Rules of NPV calculations

Include

- ✓ Effect of tax allowances
- ✓ After-tax incremental cash flows
- ✓ Working capital requirements
- ✓ Opportunity costs

Exclude

- ✗ Depreciation
- ✗ Dividend/interest payments
- ✗ Sunk costs
- ✗ Allocated costs and overheads

	Year 0	Year 1	Year 2	Year 3	Year 4	
Sales receipts		X	X	X		
Costs	___	(X)	(X)	(X)	___	
Sales less Costs		X	X	X		
Taxation		(X)	(X)	(X)	(X)	
Capital	(X)					
Scrap value				X		
Working capital	(X)			X		
Tax saved -						
Tax allowances	___	X	X	X	X	
	(X)	X	X	X	(X)	
Discount factors @						
Cost of capital (WACC)	X	X	X	X	X	NPV is the sum
Present value	(X)	X	X	X	(X)	of present values

The IRR (internal rate of return) method calculates the rate of return at which the NPV is zero.

1 Calculate net present value using rate for cost of capital which

   a Is whole number

   b May give NPV close to zero ($2/3 - 3/4$ accounting return on investment)

2 Calculate second NPV using a different rate

   a If first NPV is positive, use second rate greater than first rate

   b If first NPV is negative, use second rate less than first rate

3 Use two NPV values to calculate IRR

$$IRR = A + \frac{N_A}{N_A - N_B}(B - A)$$

where

A is lower of two rates of return used
B is higher of two rates of return used
N_A is NPV obtained using rate A
N_B is NPV obtained using rate B

NPV
■ Simpler to calculate
■ Better for ranking mutually exclusive projects
■ Easy to incorporate different discount rates

IRR
■ More easily understood
■ Can be confused with ROCE
■ Ignores relative size of investments
■ May be several IRRs if cash flows not conventional

MIRR

Assume cash inflows invested and increase in value by cost of capital multiplier. Divide these cash inflows by year 0 cash outflow to find annuity factor corresponding to MIRR.

Investment appraisal in practice

■ Most companies use payback method due to uncertainty of future cash flows and recurring pattern of flows over time

■ ARR method often used as it reflects importance of rate of return on capital

■ IRR method preferred to NPV

■ NPV method seen as too long-term and unable to incorporate all relevant factors

Money rate of return measures return in terms of the currency.

Real rate of return measures return in constant price level terms.

Formula

$(1 + \text{money rate}) = (1 + \text{real rate}) \times (1 + \text{inflation rate})$

Real rate or money rate?

- If cash flows in terms of **actual currency** received/paid on **various future dates**, use **money rates**

- If cash flows in terms of **value of pound at time 0** (constant price levels) use **real rates**

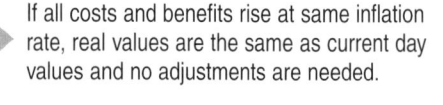

If all costs and benefits rise at same inflation rate, real values are the same as current day values and no adjustments are needed.

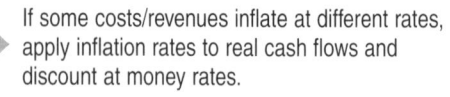

If some costs/revenues inflate at different rates, apply inflation rates to real cash flows and discount at money rates.

Working capital

Increases in working capital reduce net cash flow. Working capital is recovered at the end of the project.

Tax assumptions

- Tax is paid quarterly (half in year profits are made, half in the year afterwards) (usual assumption)

- Tax is paid in year profits are made

- Tax is paid year after profits are made

Tax and DCF

Ignore tax, use pre-tax rate of return.

Include tax, use post-tax rate of return.

Tax-allowable depreciation

Should be treated as cash saving.

Generally 25% on reducing balance (though may be 25% straight line or equal depreciation).

First claim may be at time 0 or time 1.

Tax effect will depend on tax assumptions.

When asset sold:

- Taxable profit if sale price > reducing balance

- Tax allowable loss if sale price < reducing balance

International investment appraisal

		Time				
Foreign currency cash flows	0	1	2	3	4	5
Sales receipts		X	X	X	X	
Costs		(X)	(X)	(X)	(X)	
Tax allowable depreciation		(X)	(X)	(X)	(X)	
Taxable profit		X	X	X	X	
Taxation			(X)	(X)	(X)	(X)
Tax allowable depreciation		X	X	X	X	
Capital expenditure	(X)					
Scrap value					X	
Tax on scrap value						(X)
Terminal value					X	
Tax on terminal value						(X)
Working capital	(X)	(X)	(X)	X	X	
	(X)	X	X	X	X	(X)

			Time			
	0	1	2	3	4	5
Exchange rates	X	X	X	X	X	X
Sterling cash flows						
Invested in/remitted						
from foreign country	(X)	X	X	X	X	(X)
Additional UK tax			(X)	(X)	(X)	(X)
Additional UK expenses/income		(X)	(X)	(X)	(X)	
UK tax effect of UK expenses/income			X	X	X	X
Net sterling cash flows	(X)	X	X	X	X	(X)
Discount factors @ UK%	X	X	X	X	X	X
Present values	(X)	X	X	X	X	(X)

Remember also

- Use of purchasing power parity/interest rate parity to predict future rates
- Host country currency used in order to make comparisons
- Project evaluated by funds sent to parent
- Funds can be sent by licensing fees, payments for imports
- Consider different inflation rates
- Consider different tax rates
- Problems of estimating terminal values

The discount rate used may be adjusted to take account of political or currency risk, or international portfolio diversification

Example

Current \$/£ spot rate is 1.5, UK interest rate 8%, \$ expected to appreciate against £ by annual 5%.

Forward rate \$/£ = Spot \$/£ $\times \dfrac{1 + \text{US interest rate}}{1 + \text{UK interest rate}}$

$$1.5 \times (1 - 0.05) = 1.5 \times \frac{1 + \text{US interest rate}}{1 + 0.08}$$

$$1 + \text{US interest rate} = \frac{1.425 \times 1.08}{1.5} = 1.03$$

3% will be used to evaluate \$ NPV, which will be translated at 1.5.

19: Applications of discounted cash flow

Topic List

Annualised cost of capital items

Capital rationing

Single period rationing

Real options

Adjusted present value

Dealing with uncertainty

Real options are increasingly important; watch out for articles on this issue.

Equivalent annual cost

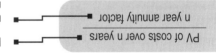

Equivalent annual cost = $\dfrac{\text{PV of costs over n years}}{\text{n year annuity factor}}$

- PV of costs is purchase cost – PV disposal proceeds
- n year annuity factor is at company's cost of capital, for number of years of item's life.

Example

Project involves capital expenditure of £100,000.
Annual revenues are £90,000, costs of £60,000 (excluding depreciation).
Equipment has seven year life, no residual value, financed by a loan at 8% interest per annum.

$$\text{Annualised cost} = \frac{£100,000}{\text{PV years 1 - 7 at 8\%}} = \frac{£100,000}{5.206} = £19,209$$

Annual profit = 100,000 – 60,000 – 19,209 = £20,791. Project is worthwhile.

Capital rationing

is where a company has a limited amount of money to invest and investments have to be compared in order to allocate money most effectively.

Soft capital rationing
Internal factors

- Reluctance to cede control
- Wish to use only retained earnings
- Reluctance to dilute EPS
- Reluctance to pay more interest
- Capital expenditure budgets

Relaxation of capital constraints

- Joint ventures
- Licensing/franchising
- Contracting out
- Other sources of finance

Hard capital rationing
External factors

- Depressed stock market
- Restrictions on bank lending
- Conservative lending policies
- Issue costs

19: Applications of discounted cash flow

Profitability index

$$PI = \frac{\text{PV cash inflows}}{\text{PV initial investment}}$$

Assumptions of PI method

- Opportunity to undertake project lost if not taken during capital rationing period
- Compare uncertainty about project outcomes
- Projects are divisible
- Ignore strategic value
- Ignore cash flow patterns
- Ignore project sizes

Single period rationing with indivisible projects

- If projects are not divisible, PI method may not give optimal solution
- Unused capital

Use trial and error and test NPV available from different combinations of projects.

Options to make follow-on investments

Investing in a project may lead to other possibilities or options which are valuable, but have not been included in the NPV calculation.

Valuation of follow-on investments

- Present value of future benefit streams
- Initial cost of follow-on project
- Time within which option exercised
- Variability of expected project returns
- Risk-free rate of interest

Option to abandon

Option to abandon could be valuable if future benefit streams are uncertain.

Option to wait

Generally there is a time period over which a project can be postponed (corresponding to option exercise period). New information may emerge that will aid decision-making.

19: Applications of discounted cash flow

The adjusted present value approach involves evaluating projects as if they were all equity financed and then adjusting for method of financing.

Step 1. For geared company, calculate cost of equity in ungeared company by using formula:

$$k_{eg} = k_{eu} + \left[k_{eu} + k_d \right] \frac{V_D (1 - 1}{V_E}$$

Where k_{eg} is cost of equity in geared company
k_{eu} is cost of equity in ungeared company
k_d is cost of debt
V_E is market value of equity
V_D is market value of debt

Step 2. Calculate NPV of project using k_{eu} as discount rate

Step 3. Establish effect of gearing on project by using

$$V_g(APV) = V_u + TB_C$$

Where MV_g is market value of geared company
TB_C is the tax shield
V_u is market value of ungeared company

Complications in APV technique

- Establishing suitable cost of equity
- Identifying all financing costs
- Choosing correct discount rates

However APV can be used to evaluate all financing effects, and is not dependent on the assumption of risk free debt.

Complications in APV calculations

- Issue costs - be careful with calculations and need to discount tax effect
- Increased debt capacity - Incremental effect is tax shield of increased debt finance
- Subsidised borrowing - Include savings in interest and tax shield effect discounted at normal cost of borrowing

Sensitivity analysis

assesses how responsive a project's NPV is to changes in the variables used to calculate the NPV.

Risk is where there are several possible outcomes, and probabilities can be assigned to outcomes on the basis of past experience.

Assess effect of changes in selling price, sales volume, cost of capital, costs and benefits.

Weaknesses

- Only considers one variable at a time
- Changes in variables often interdependent
- Takes no account of probabilities
- Critical factors possibly not controllable
- Doesn't provide decision rule

Risk reduction methods

- Maximum payback period
- High discounting rate
- Selection of projects with low standard deviation and acceptable predicted outcomes
- Attention directed to critical factors
- Use prudence/pessimistic estimates
- Certainty equivalents (convert cash flows to risk-free amounts)

Certainty equivalent approach

The certainty equivalent approach involves converting expected cash flows into equivalent risk-free amounts and discounting at the risk-free rate. The greater the risk of the expected cash flow:

- The smaller the certainty equivalent receipt
- The larger the certainty equivalent payment

Disadvantages of certainty equivalents

- Adjustments to cash flows decided subjectively
- Ascertaining the risk-free rate

Example

Ella is considering a project with the following discounted cash flows

Year	£
0	(10,000)
1	6,000
2	7,000
3	(2,000)
	1,000

Ella decides to decrease Year 1 and Year 2 receipts by 10% + 20% and increase Year 3 payment by 25% to obtain certainty equivalents

Year	£
0	(10,000)
1	5,400
2	5,600
3	(2,500)
	(1,500)

19: Applications of discounted cash flow

Probability analysis

1. Calculate expected value of NPV

2. Measure risk by one of following methods
   - Calculate worst possible outcome and its probability
   - Calculate probability that project fail to achieve positive NPV
   - Calculate standard deviation of NPV

   $$S = \sqrt{\sum p(X - \overline{X})^2}$$

   where
   - S = standard deviation
   - X = outcome
   - $\overline{X}$ = expected value
   - p = probability of outcome

Which project should be selected?

If projects are mutually exclusive and carry different levels of risk, with the less risky project having a lower expected NPV, which project is selected will depend on how risk-averse management are.

Problems with expected values
<ul><li>Investment may be one-off, and expected value not possible outcome</li><li>Assigning probabilities may be subjective</li><li>Expected values do not indicate range of outcomes</li></ul>

20: Investment and project control

Topic List

Stages and success factors

Feasibility study

Project control

This chapter summarises the main procedures organisations use to implement and control investment projects. You may have to discuss whether the procedures a particular organisation is using, or plans to use, are adequate.

Project phases

1 Initiation ⎤
2 Formation ⎬ Defining
3 Objective setting ⎦

4 Task planning ⎤
5 Feasibility ⎥
6 Fact finding ⎥
7 Position analysis ⎬ Planning
8 Options generation ⎥
9 Options evaluation ⎦

10 Design and development ⎤
11 Implementation ⎦ Implementing

12 Review ⎤
13 Completion ⎦ Controlling and completing

Project success factors

- Clearly defined mission and goals
- Top management support
- Competent project manager
- Competent team members
- Sufficient resources
- Excellent communication channels
- Clear client focus

FEASIBILITY STUDY

Operational — **Technical** — **Social** — **Ecological** — **Economic**

Feasibility study team

Team should have clear terms of reference and be drawn from the departments affected by the investments. All team members should be able to be objectively critical, and at least some should be able to assess technical and organisational implications of the proposals.

Option evaluation

Stage 1.	Create base constraints
Stage 2.	Create option outlines
Stage 3.	Assess impact on operations of relevant department/organisations
Stage 4.	Review proposals with people affected

20: Investment and project control

Project control

Key elements:

- **Organisation** - Terms of reference defining objectives, timescales, roles and resources
- **Reporting structure**
- **Overall project plan** supplemented by subsidiary plans and budgets
- **Quality standards**
- **Risk assessment** and **management**
- **Reports on progress**
- **Dealing with problems and slippage** may involve rescheduling. Implications of major changes should be carefully investigated
- **Reviewing investment success** including whether performance good or bad, purpose(s), quantitative and qualitative measures

Post-audit

is an objective and independent appraisal of the success of a capital project in progressing the business.

- Incentive for managers to consider benefits/costs
- Indicates efficiency improvements
- Identifies good/poor performers
- Identifies weaknesses in forecasting

Problems with post-audits

- Number of uncontrollable factors
- Difficult to identify costs/benefits
- Costly and time-consuming
- Managers become too risk-averse